Sunny Me

Sunny Me

Deborah Rowe Johnson Designs

ISBN 978-1-64258-520-9 (paperback)
ISBN 978-1-64258-522-3 (hardcover)
ISBN 978-1-64258-521-6 (digital)

Christian Faith Publishing, Inc.
832 Park Avenue
Meadville, PA 16335
www.christianfaithpublishing.com

"Sunny Me"

God's Reflections, Inc.®

Deborah Rowe Johnson

Illustrations by

Deborah Rowe Johnson

SUNSHINE

Happy Happy Happy
Beautiful
Joy
Light
Comes from Heaven
Hot Happens in the daytime
Great Bright
Makes us Smile
Makes us Laugh
Comes Up
Goes Down
Allows us to SEE
It is Powerful
Hot!!!!! Did I say, "HOT"!!!!!
Makes us Sweat
It's in the Sky
Takes away Sadness
It is God

From Sunny Me to Sunny You

Dear friends and readers,

I am so thankful to God for the creation of Sunny Me and
God's grace that has allowed me the ability to create and share this
fun-loving, happy sunshine character with all of you.
God created the sun for us to have light, warmth, and life in our universe.
Sunny Me is a ball of sunshine, spreading happiness and love to the world.

It is my heart's desire that you enjoy reading this book as much as I have found
pleasure in writing and creating it. I pray it brings laughter and joy to you
and all others that you share this story with.

Spreading Sunshine to all the world!

God Bless You,
Deborah Rowe Johnson

WOW

It's A

BEAUTIFUL DAY!!!!

SUNNY ☼ ME

SUNNY ME

My name is Sunny Me,
and I am going to be
Happy today!

I can be happy
because
I am healthy and bright.

God made me a big, bright sunshine
so I can be a light for other people to see
and make other people

Happppppppy tooooooooooo!!!!!!!!

SUNNY ☀ ME

This is a great day!
I WONDER
what will come my way?

?????

Will it be ice cream
or maybe

chocolate Chip
C O OKIES?

SUNNY ☀ ME

The first thing I am going to
do is thank God for
all His blessings.

Thank you, Lord, that I can
walk, talk, think,
laugh, smell, see, hear, and

do just about anything I
want to do.

The second thing I am going to do
Is MAKE MY BED because my momma loves it
when I help keep my room clean and neat.

She really goes wild when I make my bed without being told.
Yes, I mean wild ...
She starts jumping around like a bunny
Who has eaten tooooooo much chocolate!
Hee Hee.

Hippitteee Hop ... Hip It Tee Hop!

SO ... since I made my bed, do you think my
momma might get me a prize?
Do you think so?

SUNNY ☀ ME

The third thing I am going to do is pray ...
Thinking in my head right now
that God will send His angels to help my momma
find a prize for me!

Yes, it is a good day already!

Heeeeeeeeee ... Yipp-peeeee
for Sunny ME!

The fourth thing I have to do is decide
what shoes I am going to wear today.

I have to start getting ready for my big day.
I am going to be the best in my class at school.
What shoes, what shoes, oh me, oh my,
what shoes will Sunny Me wear?
HUH!!!

SUNNY ☼ ME

SUNNY ☀ ME

Yes, I've got it ...
I feel like wearing
my bright-red tennis shoes.

Wow, my red shoes are going to
be so great!!!!!

Do you like red tennis shoes too?

These shoes I have are soooo bright red, they are like Rudolph the Red-Nosed Reindeer. Do you know Rudolph? He is the leader of Santa's sleigh on Christmas Eve night. Rudolph was the only reindeer with a red light for a nose, and he used his nose to lead Santa in the dark sky. The only way Santa could see where to go was by Rudolph's nose light.

Anyway, that is how bright my tennis shoes are.
HEE HEE ... Sunny ME!

Do you know what the color red means?
RED is a POWERFUL color.

It is STRONG, and
I feel strong today!

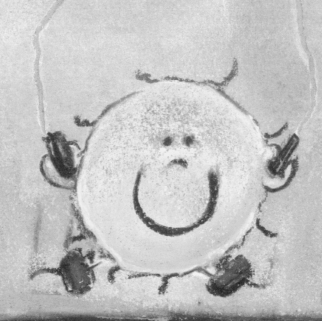

SUNNY ME JUMPING ROPE

My bright-red shoes will give me power to
be a winner,

Crush a spider,

Skip, hop, gallop, and play,
Run ... and I mean run fast!!!!!!!!!!!!

And step over anything that gets in my way today.
"Thank you, Jesus, for giving me a strong body."

SUNNY ☼ ME

I better go to the kitchen because I think
I hear Momma calling me.

Yes, that is her voice ...
"Sunny Me, what would you like for breakfast today?"

Oh boy, here I go,

"Momma, I am coming!
I will be right there."

The fifth thing I am going to do is eat a
healthy breakfast. What would be healthy?
Toast ... cereal ... eggs ... cinnamon rolls
juice ... pancakes ... oatmeal.

YUCK!!! NOT OATMEAL!!!!

Wait ... I know, I am going to eat cereal!

No.
I think eggs, toast, and orange juice!

SUNNY   ME   26

SUNNY ☀ ME

I am trying to EAT good
so I can be stronger, smarter, and real healthy.
Did you know that eggs are BRAIN FOOD?

EGGS are full of PROTEIN, and
that makes my brain work faster.

If my brain is working fast,
then I will be smarter.
I feel SMARTER already!

Hee Hee Sunny Me ... smart me.

My brain tells my body what to do and how to work.
So I need to keep it strong.

Another way I can keep my brain strong is to only have good thoughts.
When I have bad thoughts, it is like being in the dark.

I like being happy and in the light ... so I have to

THINK
HAPPY
THOUGHTS!!

I am going to pray to Jesus.
"Jesus, can you help me keep the
bad, ugly thoughts

out of my brain today ...

So I will only have GOOD THOUGHTS?"

SUNNY ☀ ME

Think **GOOD THOUGHTS** like these:

1. Today is a good day.

2. God loves me.

3. God made me.

4. God does not make any mistakes, and He created me.

5. I have a great family.

6. God gave me a great mom and dad.

7. I am smart.

8. I am strong.

Good things will come my way today
because I am blessed.

SUNNY ME

If I start feeling sad or mad ... or if bad thoughts come in my brain, then

I will just ask Jesus to take those bad things in my brain and
throw them into the lake.

I have a lake near my house, and bad thoughts
Can't swim ...

SOOOOOOO
I know bad thoughts do not have a life jacket
and will drown in the lake.

Now I do not have to be afraid of them anymore.
💜 Jesus loves me and will keep me safe.

We say, "GET OUT OF HERE, Nasty THOUGHTS,
In JESUS NAME."

Wow, I sure do love these eggs and toast.

I wish I could have 100 pieces of toast with jelly today,

But ... I guess I better hurry up and get moving
because I hear the big school bus coming outside!!!

SUNNY ME

The sixth thing I need to do is
GO back upstairs to brush my teeth.

Dr. Boyd is my dentist,
and he thinks I do a good job brushing my teeth.
I did not have one cavity the last time I went to the dentist.

I brush my teeth every morning before school and
every night before bed.
Do you brush your teeth every day?

It keeps my teeth white. It makes my breath smell like peppermint candy,
and people like to talk to me more.

Hey ... brushing my teeth gives me more friends!!!

That is a wonderful thing ... do you want more friends?

I have brushed my teeth, and now I am off to a good start.
The last thing I am going to do is
pray I have a great day.

Dear God,
Thank you for your grace that you pour over me
Like honey
and that you love me
no matter what.

IS GRACE LIKE squirting a bunch of honey out of
the bottle over the top of my head
and letting it run down the back of my neck?
Huh???
HONEY on my head and running down my neck???

It SOUNDS

STICKY!

Well, the Bible says, GRACE is FROM GOD.
It's A FREE GIFT FROM GOD.

Grace IS
Like the biggest birthday box you can dream of!!!!
Just for you
But it is not your birthday.

God just wants to give you His love all the time,
every day … all day long.

It is sweet as HONEY.

Isn't God the Best Ever?

SUNNY ☼ ME

GIFTS

♥ ♥   ♥ ♥

sunny
me

Finally, I am riding the school bus to O'Hagan Elementary.
God is going to show me big things today!

I know I will see sunshine all day.
Oh me ... Oh my

Yes ... SUNNY ME.

SUNNY ☀ ME

I HOPE YOU HAVE A GOOD DAY TOO.
I PASS ON MY SUNSHINE TO YOU.

SOOOOOOOO ... we say,

sunny you

Sign your NAME:_____

Sunny Me

For all the world to see…
sunshine, hope, love, and unity.
Sunny Me has been birthed
to bring laughter and love to all.
The foundation of Sunny Me
Is God's Reflections, Inc.
May we all be reminded by this happy
sunshine character that
God is our Creator, and we are all
God's Reflections!

Spreading light to all the world

God's Reflections, Inc.®

About the Author

Deborah R. Johnson was born in Joplin, Missouri, in 1965, an identical twin, and a family of five. She moved to Temple, Texas, at the age of twelve and has been a native Texan ever since. She is a graduate of Southwest Texas State University with a Bachelor of Science in exercise physiology, health and nutrition. She is married to Toby Johnson and has been a teacher and coach for twenty-five years. This experience has enlightened her to create a fun-loving happy character for children and adults to enjoy. The Lord has blessed her with the gift of writing and painting, and her business is called God's Reflections, Inc. Janice Rowe, Deborah's mother, spoke this business and knowledge of writing and painting into existence. If Deborah did not know the Lord and believe in his promises, this would have been unbelievable and probably nonexistent venture. She is thankful to the Lord for wisdom, faith, and the direction to study the Word in courses of study with Billy Graham Evangelist Association. This study has given her the knowledge needed to reveal the importance of spreading the good news, hope, and love to people all around the world. It is Deborah's prayer that Sunny Me touches the lives of many and inspires a desire to spread light and read more of God's Reflections books, greeting cards, and journals in the future. We are all God's Reflections, and she hopes that this book is an inspiration of light to all nationalities.